The Evil Eye
of Gondôr

A Play for Children

Bryan Owen

GW00504088

Samuel French – London
New York – Sydney – Toronto – Hollywood

© 1983 BY BRYAN OWEN

This play is fully protected under the Copyright Laws of the British Commonwealth of Nations, the United States of America and all countries of the Berne and Universal Copyright Conventions.

All rights, including Stage, Motion Picture, Radio, Television, Public Reading, and Translation into Foreign Languages, are strictly reserved.

No part of this publication may lawfully be transmitted, stored in a retrieval system, or reproduced in any form or by any means, electronic, mechanical, photocopying, manuscript, typescript, recording, or otherwise, without the prior permission of the copyright owners.

Rights of Performance by Amateurs are controlled by SAMUEL FRENCH LTD, 26 SOUTHAMPTON STREET, LONDON WC2E 7JE, and they, or their authorized agents, issue licences to amateurs on payment of a fee. **It is an infringement of the Copyright to give any performance or public reading of the play before the fee has been paid and the licence issued.**

Licences are issued subject to the understanding that it shall be made clear in all advertising matter that the audience will witness an amateur performance; that the names of the authors of the plays shall be included on all announcements and on all programmes; and that the integrity of the author's work will be preserved.

The Royalty Fee indicated below is subject to contract and subject to variation at the sole discretion of Samuel French Ltd

> Basic fee for each and every
> performance by amateurs   Code G
> in the British Isles

In Theatres or Halls seating Six Hundred or more the fee will be subject to negotiation.

In Territories Overseas the fee quoted above may not apply. A fee will be quoted on application to our local authorized agent, or if there is no such agent, on application to Samuel French Ltd, London.

The publication of this play does not imply that it is necessarily available for performance by amateurs or professionals, either in the British Isles or Overseas. Amateurs and professionals considering a production are strongly advised in their own interests to apply to the appropriate agents for consent before starting rehearsals or booking a theatre or hall.

ISBN 0 573 05066 X

THE EVIL EYE OF GONDÔR

A long time ago there was a beautiful Valley. It was green and pleasant, and home to lots of nice people who lived in villages like Little Brumley, which was near the forest, and Upper Lonsdale, which was up in the northern reaches.

Unfortunately, other people lived in the Valley too, and they weren't very nice at all. They were the Guardians of the Eye of Gondôr . . .

No-one knows when the Eye arrived in the little Valley. In fact, no-one knows very much about it at all, except that it had been there ever since the Ancient Times, and all those years the people had lived in the shadow of its evil power.

One Harvest-time, when Roth was the most wicked Guardian of all, a Stranger arrived, just as it had been written a long time before. This is the story of what happened then . . . and still happens now . . . in little valleys all over the world . . .

Bryan Owen
Deal, England 1982

THE PEOPLE OF THE VALLEY

The People
It's some years since I first went to the Valley but if you're going to tell their story let me tell you something about the people who lived there. It's strange, you see, because they're so different from us and yet . . . well . . . in some ways they're much the same. Except the **Guardians**, that is. I mean, no-one can be quite like the **Guardians**. It makes me shudder even to think of them!

They lived in the Castle of Gondôr, a dark, bleak place that housed the **Evil Eye**, but there was no place in the whole Valley safe from its terrible power. The **Guardians** themselves dressed in purple robes and black cloaks, although **Roth**, the most senior Guardian of all, the master of the secrets of the Eye, wore a black robe and purple cloak. They all wore dark masks—helmets that came halfway down their faces, frightening and fearful.

The **Guardians** also had weapons—staves, in fact. They were painted red which matched the redness of the table in the castle. Of course, **Roth**'s staff was longer and more ornately carved than the others, and I noticed that he also wore a decorated belt which made him look much more important.

On the other hand, the **Mayor** was a friendly character but ever so fussy. Black and white were his favourite colours because they were formal. He liked to wear a top hat and, of course, Little Brumley's mayoral chain of office, something he wore with pride.

The **Storyteller** was the most friendly character I met, and his clothes really stood out from the rest. I remember he wore a large floppy hat with a yellow feather in it and he carried around a brightly coloured broom! It was really rather fine.

The **Villagers** were very poor and suffered terribly under **Roth**, so their colours were much more subdued—browns, for example. It was much the same for the **Outlaws** although they managed some greens, seeing that they lived in the forest. In point of fact, most of their clothes were tattered and torn, and the repairs that they did do weren't very good.

Mack stood out, though, and **Big Harry**, when I met him, was the smallest outlaw of all wearing the baggiest pair of shorts he could find. **Will** and **Stout** wore almost identical clothing, but I suppose that was because they were brothers.

The **Stranger**—well, he was an enigma. I mean, no-one knew where he came from, and he'd been travelling for half a year. His clothes were different. And he didn't wear an eye badge either—that was asking for trouble, which is precisely what happened! When I met him that first time he turned up in a white robe, barefooted and carrying a staff. He had a purple sash, a purple cloak and the cut of his clothes, would you believe, rather reminded me of **Roth** himself? A bit strange, that, when you come to think of it.

The **Monsters** turned up on one occasion but it was dark and I really can't remember much about them. They were really weird, but when you think about it they were only illusions created by **Roth** anyway . . .

Telling the story . . .
Members of the audience are always made to feel welcome in Little Brumley. That means that as soon as they've arrived they are greeted by the Mayor and maybe one or two Villagers. He is fussy, though, and may well tell people like Will and Stout off if they don't show people to their seats in a polite and friendly way.

On stage everyone is taking a break after the labours of the day. I mean, after all's said and done, it is the day of the harvest, isn't it? In fact, they've stopped off at a secret place to meet with the Outlaws, just to chat mainly, and perhaps play dice, or talk about the dance. It's quite possible that members of the audience can overhear them as they exchange news and comment on the harvest, wondering whether the Guardians are going to come this year. Depending when the doors open this might go on for half an hour before, imperceptibly, the action moves into the first scene and the lights go down.

This friendliness continues, of course, during the Interval. The Storyteller, maintaining the friendly traditions of the people of Little Brumley, usually tells the audience of Brumley Brew which is on sale on the stage and served by the Villagers and Outlaws. Although he doesn't want to he also has to tell the audience about Castle Coffee which is sold by the Guardians nearby. Only the bravest of adults volunteer to go anywhere near *them*.

While all this is going on the Mayor feels that it is most important that he continues to talk to people, telling them the history of the Valley, and doing his best to avoid Roth who's going around being quite, quite nasty.

As you know, some of the Villagers and Outlaws love to dance. They are probably even practising for the dance tomorrow night—dances like the Circassian Circle, for instance. Sometimes I've even known members of the audience to join in!

THE ANCIENT WRITINGS
The people of Little Brumley are the friendliest people I know. It's not their fault that the Guardians spoil things for them, and when they get together with a little bit of help from the Stranger they can overcome their fear and become what they are meant to become. It was all written a long time ago, of course, in the ancient writings. The trouble is that these days people don't read the Ancient Writings any more. I mean, just because they're old doesn't mean to say that they're not true, does it?

No doubt you know as well as I do that it's hard to break away from old habits. The Mayor found exactly that. It was a big step forward for a man so afraid. But the greater our fear the bigger our steps have to be.

I've met the Stranger lots of times since I first saw him in Little Brumley. He's always on the move, he goes where he will, and he's full of surprises. If you keep your eyes open, and look very carefully, I think you'll see him coming . . .

                                                                Bryan Owen

ACKNOWLEDGEMENTS

THE EVIL EYE OF GONDÔR was first produced by t   matic Society at Dover Grammar School for Boys in November 1981 with the following cast to whom the play is dedicated:

Lee Abbott, Daniel Beard, Kevin Black, Philip Buddle, Ralph Buddle*, Chris Button*, Mark Castle, Neil Castle, Paul Castle, Fraser Chatburn, Neil Cox*, Geoff Dale*, Paul Gilliott, Andrew Hedgecock*, Chris Hook, Steve Howard, Mark Jones, Andrew Marsh, John Merenith*, Paul Muir, Damion Napier*, Stuart Napier, Chris Newall, Mark Newall, Stephen Oliver, Robert Osborn, Mark Pocknall, Andrew Pope, Danny Rees, Marcus Ripley, Kevin Streater, David Willoughby*.

* Members of the National Youth Theatre of Great Britain

My thanks also go to Deborah Roberts who helped with the school production, and to Mary Quinton, not only for her help with many productions over the years but also for a great deal of encouragement when life at school grew unbearable, support was in short supply and I felt like giving up.

CHARACTERS

Will, a village boy
Stout, Will's brother
The Mayor
The Storyteller
The Stranger, a traveller
First Villager
Second Villager
Third Villager
Roth, the Master of the Guardians
Brasov, the Guardian gaoler
Kafka, a Guardian
Martin, a prisoner
Rowan, a prisoner
Jonah, a young outlaw
Scamp, a young outlaw
Big Harry, an outlaw
Mack, leader of the outlaws
First Outlaw
Second Outlaw
Third Outlaw
Villagers
Outlaws
Guardians
Monsters

ACT I

SCENE 1

The Market Square at Little Brumley

Villagers, including the Storyteller, are carrying sacks, farm implements and other things to suggest the harvest. All wear the badge of the Eye of Gondôr

Will, a village boy, enters, carrying some tools

Will (*calling*) Come on, Stout! Where are you?

Stout enters, pulling a sack

Stout (*panting*) Hold on . . . not so fast! I can't keep up with you, Will.

Will If we don't get a move on we'll be late home for supper, and you know what our mum's like if we keep her cooking waiting.

Stout You wouldn't be so fast if you had to carry this sack. It's all right for you, you're only carrying the tools. Here—you have the sack and I'll take the hoe.

Will You want to go to the dance tomorrow night, don't you?

Stout Yeah!

Will You want to make a good impression on Mistress Lucy, don't you?

Stout Yeah!

Will You want to be handsome and debonair like me, don't you? (*He preens himself*)

Stout Yeah! Well, er, handsome and debonair, yes. But not like you . . .

Will Well, carrying the sack will help you get some of that weight off. What we need now is the new, improved, slimline Stout . . . then Mistress Lucy won't be able to resist you. With you as fat as you are, she couldn't even get within hailing distance!

Stout (*upset*) Now, Will. Just you stop that. (*He hits out at Will*)

Will evades Stout's blow and dodges away. Stout chases after him but is unable to catch him

You promised you wouldn't make fun of me. (*Still chasing after Will*) Hey! Come here!

Eventually, Stout collapses on his sack, out of breath

Will I'm sorry, Stout, but you really have only yourself to blame. You eat too much and you work too little.

Stout Ah, but Mum's cooking is the best in Little Brumley—in all the Valley I shouldn't wonder. Only yesterday the Mayor came up to me and said he'd never tasted better.

Will The Mayor? When did he come and eat our mum's cooking?

Stout Ah! He came when you were off courtin' Mistress—

Will I was doing no such thing!

Stout —courtin' Mistress Marion. I 'eard tell you were 'oldin' 'ands down Duck Lane. I 'eard tell you then went round the back of the pond. I 'eard tell that you and Mistress Marion then—

Will Never mind what you heard tell! It's not true!

Stout If you promise not to make fun of me then I won't say what I 'eard tell you and Mistress Marion were seen doin' next . . .

Will All right! I promise!

Stout Cross your 'eart and 'ope to die?

Will Cross my heart and hope to die.

Stout Hey, Will . . .

Will What?

Stout (*daringly*) Was it nice?

Will Was what nice?

Stout What you were doin' with Mistress Marion?

Will Stout! You promised!

Stout All right! We'd better be gettin' these things 'ome. Your turn to carry the sack.

Will Oh no. I'm carrying the tools. If you want to find out . . . er . . . what you want to find out, your best bet is with Mistress Lucy at the dance tomorrow night. So you can carry the sack!

Will and Stout exit

The Mayor enters

Mayor Hurry up, everybody, get along home. (*To some of the Villagers*) Hurry up now, nearly time for curfew. Come along. (*Fussing at other Villagers*) Now, now, you can sit down when you get home. You don' want the Guardians to catch you out after curfew, do you?

The Villagers get up and, as they move to leave, they freeze—all except the Storyteller

Storyteller Hello everybody. Welcome to our valley. This is Little Brumley. I see you've met Will and Stout already. They're nice lads, work hard now that their father has gone. Mind you, they're looking forward to tomorrow night. Today's the last day of the harvest. And tomorrow? Tomorrow's the biggest and best dance of the year! Everyone in the village will be there. So will Mistress Marion and Mistress Lucy, that's why Will and Stout are so excited. I'll let you into a secret! I've got my eyes on Mistress Rachel! She's the loveliest girl in the whole valley—at least, that's what I think! Mmmmmm! Oh! Where was I? Oh yes. I was telling you about the village. We're a friendly lot here really. We don't do anybody any harm. We have to be careful you see, on account of the Guardians. (*He shudders*) Keep out of their way if I was you. Hey! I can't stop around here talking to you all day. As the Mayor was saying, it's nearly curfew and we don't want trouble from the Guardians the night before the dance. I'd best be getting home. I'll see you later in the story!

The Storyteller picks up his sack and the other Villagers come to life

Mayor Come on, everybody. Get along home! (*He continues to fuss*)

The Stranger enters

Stranger Ah . . . hello. Could anyone tell me where I might spend the night?

There is consternation among the Villagers

What's the matter? I only asked if there was anywhere to spend the night. It's getting dark.

Mayor (*nervously*) Did you say "spend the night", sir?

Stranger That's right. Anywhere will do really: kitchen floor, old barn, even a shed if you've got one.

1st Villager You can't spend the night 'ere.

Mayor No-one ever spends the night here, sir.

Stranger No-one? What about all of you? Don't you spend the night here?

Mayor Oh yes, sir . . . We do . . . but what I mean to say is that . . . no-one else ever does.

1st Villager If I were you, mate, I'd be off and no mistake. You'll get yourself into trouble.

2nd Villager And all of the rest of us too. Be off with you!

Mayor I'm sorry, sir. What we mean is . . . that we don't get any . . . er . . . visitors in this valley. We . . . er . . . just don't get them . . . if you see what I mean, that is.

1st Villager And we don't want 'em. Strangers mean trouble!

2nd Villager And we don't want trouble!

3rd Villager If the Guardians catch you here you'll end up in the Castle.

2nd Villager In the dungeons!

1st Villager If the Guardians catch you 'ere likely as not some of us will end up in the dungeons too!

Stranger Guardians? Who are the Guardians?

Mayor Come along, sir. Don't trouble yourself. You really ought to be going . . . for all our sakes, if you see what I mean, sir. (*To the others*) Come along, everybody. Get along home. It's nearly curfew. We don't want any trouble tonight.

Stranger Curfew? Guardians? Why are you all so afraid? And where's this Castle? Who lives there?

Mayor I'm sorry, sir, but we're not allowed to talk to strangers. If we're caught we'll be taken away, sir.

Stranger What's the name of this Castle?

Mayor Gondôr, sir. The Castle of Gondôr . . .

1st Villager My brother was taken there last year!

2nd Villager And my uncle!

3rd Villager There's not a family in the valley that hasn't had someone taken up there.

1st Villager And they're never seen again!

2nd Villager That's why we want you to go!

1st Village Before some more are taken!

Mayor In fact, sir, I'm surprised you got this far. The Guardians don't ever let anybody cross our borders. And they don't let anybody get out, either. If I were you, sir, I'd get away from here as soon as you can, sir . . . for your own good. If they catch you, it'll mean death for you and, like as not, trouble for all of us too. I don't mean any disrespect, sir, but we have to be so careful, you see. Now, if you'll excuse us, sir, we'll all be getting off home. It's been a very hard day. Good night to you, sir.

1st Villager Be off with you!

2nd Villager And don't . . . come . . . back . . .

There is an eerie noise and the light fades

All It's the Guardians! Watch out! Aaaah! etc.

The Guardians enter wearing black cloaks and masks

The Stranger hides

The following action is played in slow motion: the Guardians begin to take the Villagers' bundles and sacks; when the Villagers protest they are thrown off; there are screams and there is wailing; all through the action there should be throbbing, menacing music and dull, mysterious lighting

When the Guardians have taken all the harvest they leave as suddenly as they came

The noise fades and the lights revert to normal. The Stranger comes out of hiding

1st Villager They've taken everything!

2nd Villager They haven't left a scrap!

3rd Villager Is anybody missing? Have they taken anybody?

2nd Villager No, we're all here. It looks like they came just for the harvest this time.

1st Villager This time! Next time it'll be one of us! It's all your fault, Stranger! We told you to go and you wouldn't!

Mayor Calm down everybody, calm down. Oh dear. It's not the Stranger's fault . . . they come every harvest time, don't they?

2nd Villager But they don't usually take all of it. There's not a scrap left! We've got nothing left for the winter.

There is silence for a moment

Stranger So they are the Guardians?

Mayor Yes, sir. Now you see why we have to be so careful.

Stranger But who are they, Mr Mayor?

Mayor They control the Valley, sir. They're the Guardians of the Eye of Gondôr.

Stranger The Eye of Gondôr?

Mayor It's the Eye that gives them power, you see, sir. Power and authority.

1st Villager It's always been like that.

2nd Villager Ever since the Ancient Times.

Mayor You see, sir, the Guardians have always controlled our Valley.

3rd Villager They're the Masters.
1st Villager And we do as we're told.
2nd Villager We keep our noses clean.
3rd Villager That way we keep out of trouble.
Stranger But they've taken your harvest—and they take it every year, you said.
1st Villager Yes, well that's the way it is, and we don't want you or anyone else sticking their noses in and causing more trouble. We've got enough already!

A bell tolls slowly in the distance. The lights fade to twilight

Mayor Curfew! That's the curfew! My, oh my! (*Panicking*) We're going to be late! I'm sorry, sir! We have to go! Good night, sir. Good night.

The Villagers and the Mayor exit

Stranger (*calling after them*) But what about me?

The Mayor returns

Mayor I'm sorry, sir. You'll have to do as best you can. But stay clear of the Guardians, sir. Stay clear of the Guardians!

The Mayor exits, hurriedly

Stranger Yes, I'll do that! I'll stay clear! (*Shouting*) I won't go near them! The trouble is, where am I going to spend the night? I daren't stay out in the open, that's for sure.
Will (*off*) Pssst!

The Stranger looks round

(*off*) Pssst!

The Stranger looks in the opposite direction to where Will and Stout are, heads visible, one above the other, at the side of the stage

(*off*) Pssst!
Stranger (*seeing him*) Who are you?

Will tiptoes on stage

Will Sssh! Not so loud! You don't want to be heard do you?

Stout creeps on

Stout Yes. You don't want to be heard.
Stranger Well, well. Who are you, then?
Will I'm Will.
Stout And I'm Stout!
Stranger I can see that, but what's your name?

Will tries to stifle a laugh

Stout (*hurt*) That *is* my name, if you please.
Stranger I'm sorry. What are you doing here, though? Aren't you afraid of being caught?

Will We're all right for a while. The Guardians have just gone back to the Castle with our harvest. They'll be too busy to bother with us just now.

Stout I hope.

Will What are you doing here?

Stout Yes, what are you doing here?

Stranger Ah, you want to know what I'm doing here!

Will hits Stout with his hat

What I'm doing immediately is looking for somewhere to spend the night. Do you have any suggestions?

Will Well, I don't know. You can't spend it in the village, that's for sure.

Stout No, you can't spend it in the vill—

Will (*interrupting*) Stout! (*To the Stranger*) Your best bet is the forest.

Stout With the Outlaws.

Will Near the marsh.

Stout With the Outlaws.

Will You'll be safe there.

Stout With the Outlaws.

Will hits Stout again with his hat

Stranger Outlaws, you say? Why should I be safe with them?

Will Because they're against the Guardians, that's why.

Stout They're our friends, the Outlaws.

Will They've gone to the forest to escape imprisonment at Gondôr.

Stout The forest is the only place where they're safe from the Guardians.

Will It's the only place where the Guardians can't venture.

Stranger How do you know all this?

Will Our father is their leader, that's how. Come on, follow me. Stout, you bring up the rear.

They all exit, tiptoeing, Stout being the most nervous

The Lights fade to a Black-out

SCENE 2

The Castle of Gondôr

An evil place, the Castle is dark and eerie. The Eye of Gondôr is upstage centre. Roth is standing in front of the Eye which throbs and glows and fades

Roth Well may you throb; well may you glow. You have brought me power, but the illusion is frail. I fear, in my bones I fear. I don't know why but there's a shadow over me and thin, boney fingers seem to be clutching at my throat. And yet why should I fear? It's the Valley that should fear me! I am Roth! I am the Master of Gondôr! Why should I fear? (*Quietly*) Yet I do ... and I don't know why ...

Brasov enters, a strong and fearsome man, the Guardian gaoler

Brasov My Lord Roth ...

Roth What is it?

Brasov The new prisoners, the ones from the northern villages, have arrived.

Roth Have you shown them to their ... accommodation?

Brasov Yes, my Lord.

Roth Good ... very good. We'll keep them out of harm's way and ... perhaps learn a little more about those dogs in the forest. Brasov ... what is the latest news about the Outlaws?

Brasov Not much, my Lord. There are now above two score hiding in the forest ...

Roth Where they're safe from our power! Do you realize, Brasov, that we are threatened while they roam free? How can we have total mastery over this Valley while there are above twenty men who deny our authority?

Brasov They still wear the Eye, my Lord.

Roth Yes, but how long will they continue to fear us if we cannot get near them? No, we must find a way to lure them out into the open, Brasov ... and perhaps I know how we can do it. Go, see to our new guests. Make sure they are ... comfortable. And, Brasov ...

Brasov Yes, my Lord?

Roth Don't take too long in finding out what we need to know ...

Brasov No, my Lord.

Brasov exits

Roth New prisoners! This is not the way to power. Soon the Castle will be full of prisoners ... what then? Who will sow corn then? Who will tend the sheep? A castle full of prisoners is a castle full of empty bellies to feed. I am trapped! The Outlaws are growing in strength. Two score now ... what next month? Three score? All the time they are free the people will see in them hope. I must crush that hope! But I must crush it without destroying the Valley. Dead villagers pay no taxes, neither do they produce any food. (*Turning to the Eye*) Oh, Eye of Gondôr ... we have work to do in this Valley. The illusion must not fail. It must not be discovered ...

Kafka, a Guardian, enters

Roth Ah, Kafka! What news?

Kafka We have brought in the harvest as you commanded, my Lord.

Roth Is there plenty?

Kafka Yes, my Lord. It has been a good summer. We shall not starve.

Roth Don't be so sure, Kafka. New prisoners were taken today from the northern villages. They have to be fed. I need to know more about the Outlaws. I fear a rising.

Kafka My Lord. I heard rumours in the Valley today.

Roth Rumours? What rumours?

Kafka About a stranger.

Roth A stranger? What stranger?

Kafka No-one knows who he is or where he comes from.

Roth A mystery, Kafka. I don't like mysteries. We must find out who he is and why he has come into the Valley. He could be very, very dangerous.

Tonight, Kafka, return to the Valley and find out what you can. I need to know who this man is!

Kafka Yes, my Lord.

Roth And Kafka ... if you get the chance ... kill him!

Kafka exits

Roth A stranger? Our borders are sealed. How could a stranger enter the Valley unseen? Maybe he is no mere man ...?

Brasov enters with Martin and Rowan, two prisoners, and a prison guard

Brasov (*to the prisoners*) Down you dogs! On your knees.

Martin and Rowan kneel

My Lord Roth, these are two of the prisoners brought from the northern villages.

Roth Are they, indeed? You are comfortable, I hope? Welcome to Gondôr. I do trust your stay will be a memorable one ...

Brasov My Lord, they have a story about ... a stranger. Seen in the north a week ago.

Roth A stranger! Ah! You are welcome indeed! Who are you?

The prisoners refuse to speak. Brasov hits them

Martin Aaaah! My name's Martin!

Roth (*to Rowan*) And you?

Rowan I will not speak!

Brasov hits Rowan

I will not speak!

Roth A foolhardy young man. Brasov ...?

Brasov continues to hit Rowan

Rowan Aaaah! All right! Aaaah! My name's Rowan, and I come from Upper Lonsdale!

Roth Upper Lonsdale? A pretty place if I'm not mistaken? Of course, I've only been there at night, you understand. Lonsdale? Lonsdale? If I remember rightly, your village is the one nearest to the northern pass, am I right?

There is no response

No matter. But the high northern pass is, of course, the border, and Upper Lonsdale would be the first village any ... er ... stranger would come to should one try to enter our little Valley?

There is no response

Now, Brasov here tells me that you have some news of such a stranger. I should very much like to hear that news.

Brasov moves as if to further hurt the prisoners

No Brasov. Our two friends lack a certain amount of, shall we say, respect!
Stand up ... and look this way ...

*Roth moves behind the Eye; the two prisoners stand. The Eye begins to glow and
fade, throbbing, accompanied by a sound which grows in intensity. The general
lighting fades and the two prisoners clap their hands over their ears. They begin
to collapse*

Know the power of the Eye of Gondôr! Know the power of Roth, the
Master of Gondôr!

*More Guardians enter and advance on the prisoners, creating a fearful
spectacle*

*Gradually the noise subsides and the Lights come up. Martin and Rowan are in
a state of collapse on the floor*

The other Guardians leave

Now, what do you know about the Stranger?

Martin (*very frightened*) He came to the village about a week ago! He asked
for some food and drink for his journey and then he went on his way.
That's all.

Roth No, there's more. Rowan of Lonsdale ... speak!

Rowan I don't know! I don't know!

Roth Speak! What is his name?

Rowan He didn't give his name!

Roth Where did he come from?

Rowan He didn't say!

Roth Where did he come from?

Rowan I don't know! I don't know! He just said he'd been travelling for a
long time!

Roth How long?

Rowan Half a year.

Roth And why did he come to our Valley? Of all valleys, why did he come to
this one?

Rowan He didn't say! He didn't say! I don't know why he came!

Roth And you, Martin of Lonsdale? Why did he come? Speak!

Martin He didn't say, he ...

Roth He what? Speak!

Martin He said that it was written long ago.

Roth Written long ago? By whom?

Martin I don't know. He didn't say. He just said that it was written.

Roth What else did he say? Come on, speak!

Martin Nothing else! He took some food and drink and went on his way. We
haven't seen him since.

Roth (*to Brasov*) Written? What writing is he referring to?

Brasov I've never heard of any such writings, my Lord.

Roth Neither have I, but that doesn't mean they don't exist. Has Kafka left
yet?

Brasov Not yet, my Lord.

Roth Come with me, let's find him. He's got work to do. Leave these two here.

Roth and Brasov exit, Roth whispering to the guard on the way out

Martin and Rowan are now alone with the guard

Rowan Martin! Martin! Are you all right?

Martin Yes, what about you?

Rowan Just a little shaken up, that's all.

Martin What do you think happened?

Rowan I don't know. The Eye glowed and there was that noise. Then everything went round and round.

Martin I feel sick.

Rowan Me too, but never mind about that. We've got to get out of here.

Martin Get out? No-one's ever got out of the Castle, you know that. We'll never get out. Never.

Rowan Don't talk like that! You've got to hope. If we lose that we lose everything. Now . . . think. We've got to find a way to give them the slip.

Martin Rowan, I don't feel very well.

Rowan Martin! (*He pauses*) Martin! Maybe that's it! If you feign sickness maybe we can knock out that guard over there.

Martin We'll never do it! And what about the Eye? It's watching us, I can feel it.

Rowan It's quiet now. Maybe it's resting. Maybe it's asleep. We'll just have to take the chance. Now, are you willing to have a go? It's either that or spend the rest of our lives in the dungeons.

Martin No, Rowan, I'm scared.

Rowan Oh, come on, Martin. What have we to lose?

Martin I dread to think. All right. What are we going to do?

Rowan There's a good lad. Now you collapse and pretend you're in pain. Leave the rest to me.

Martin collapses and moans in pain. Rowan tries to help him and becomes very worried. He looks round and sees the guard

My friend's ill! Can you help?

The guard stands impassively. Rowan continues to shout and plead

What's the matter, Martin? (*Quietly*) Keep it up, he's getting worried. (*To the guard*) I think he's dying. Can you help me?

The guard continues to stand impassively

(*Quietly*) I'll have to try something else! (*To the guard*) Guard! There's something else my friend knows about the Stranger. If he dies Roth will never find out!

At this the guard becomes concerned, looks about, and moves down towards the prisoners

Guard (*to Rowan*) Stand back!

The guard looks at Martin, and then bends over him. As he does so Martin grabs him and Rowan jumps on him. A struggle ensues, ending with the guard being knocked out. They take his cloak and sword

Rowan Now ... to escape.

Martin How are we going to do that?

Rowan Did you overhear Roth? He mentioned someone called Kafka about to leave the Castle. It's getting dark ... we'll see if we can slip out behind him.

Martin We'll never make it!

Rowan It's our only chance. They'll never be expecting it. As you said, no-one's ever escaped from the Castle before. So long as we keep to the shadows we'll get away.

Martin And if we do where will we go? They'll be looking for us. We can't go to Lonsdale.

Rowan There's only one place we can go.

Martin Where's that?

Rowan The forest ... and the Outlaws. Come on.

Martin and Rowan exit

Roth and Brasov enter quietly

Roth Perfect!

Brasov I don't quite understand, my Lord.

Roth You heard them say they're going to the forest?

Brasov Yes, my Lord.

Roth Well, if my little idea works correctly we may be able to encourage the Outlaws to leave the forest. If those two fools tell them how easy it was to escape then the Outlaws might think about an attack—in the open. Then we'll have all of them!

Roth and Brasov exit

The Lights fade to a Black-out

SCENE 3

The Forest. The Outlaws' camp. Evening

The Outlaws are mostly working—some darning clothes, some making weapons. Jonah and Scamp are peeling potatoes

Jonah Why do I always get this job? There's nothing worse than peeling potatoes.

Scamp I don't know why you're complaining. I've been spud-bashing every day this week.

Jonah With all that practice why are you so slow? Get a move on or we'll be here all night.

Scamp Don't get yourself worked up, Jonah Huggins! You're not fast yourself. You peel off more than you save.

Jonah Don't.

Scamp Do! You're the only person I know who can turn a spud into a chip just by peeling it.

Jonah Hey! You take that back or I'll thump you one.

Scamp (*standing*) Go on, then. I dare you!

Jonah (*standing*) All right, then. You asked for it!

Jonah swings at Scamp, missing him completely. He turns and they begin to scrap. Big Harry approaches

Big Harry That's enough, you two! That's enough! Come on, break it up. We've enough problems with the Guardians without you two giving us more. (*Shaking them*) Now, stop it!

There is a sullen silence

Are you finished, or do you want a hiding from me?

There is silence

Eh?

Jonah Sorry, Harry.

Scamp Yeah. Sorry.

Big Harry Now, shake hands and get back to work.

Jonah and Scamp shake hands

Go on, back to work

The potato peeling is resumed

Scamp I wonder what they're doing back in Little Brumley now?

Jonah Peeling potatoes, I shouldn't wonder.

Scamp You're complaining again.

Jonah Why shouldn't they be peeling potatoes? It's evening, isn't it? They eat the same as we do, don't they?

Scamp Of course they do. What I mean is—it's the dance tomorrow night. They'll be getting ready for it, won't they? Mum'll be baking cakes, the lads'll be decorating the village hall, old Mr Bagshot'll be tuning up his fiddle. I wish I were back at Little Brumley.

Jonah Better there than at Upper Lonsdale, I'd say. Did you hear about the trouble they had?

Scamp When that Stranger came?

Jonah Yeah. Weird, isn't it? I mean, no-one knew who he was. He sort of came from nowhere.

Scamp I'd leave well alone if I were you, Jonah Huggins! I don't suppose the Guardians were very pleased when they heard about it, and we've got enough trouble keeping out of their way here in the forest without worrying about what's been going on in the northern reaches.

Jonah Still, it's very strange. They say he wasn't even wearing his Eye.

Scamp I heard that too. Dangerous if you ask me.

Jonah But I never heard of anyone not wearing his Eye. Everybody wears his Eye. It's the law, isn't it?

Scamp It's the law, all right. If the Guardians catch him he'll be for the Castle. He's got trouble coming, whoever he is.

Jonah Here's Mack, maybe he's got some news!

Mack, the leader of the Outlaws, enters

All Hello, Mack! Any news? How's Little Brumley? *etc*

Mack Gather round, everyone! Gather round!

The Outlaws gather round to hear what Mack has to say

There was trouble in Little Brumley last night. The Guardians came.

There is consternation among the Outlaws

1st Outlaw What happened, Mack? Anyone hurt?

2nd Outlaw Did they take anyone away?

Mack No, they didn't take anyone this time. But they did take the harvest.

3rd Outlaw The harvest? All of it?

Mack Yes, as far as I can make out. They took the lot.

Big Harry They've never taken all of it before. They've always left us something!

1st Outlaw What's everyone goin' to live on through the winter?

2nd Outlaw They'll all starve!

1st Outlaw What are we goin' to do, Mack?

Mack What can we do? They're the Guardians.

3rd Outlaw We've got to do something. We can't let our families starve.

1st Outlaw And if they starve we starve too, remember.

Big Harry That's right! We depend on them, Mack.

Mack And they depend on us. Don't forget that. If we get caught what hope will our families have then?

1st Outlaw Hey! Listen! Someone's coming!

The Outlaws prepare to take cover

Martin and Rowan enter

Rowan Oh! You must be the Outlaws?

Mack Some call us that. Who might you be?

Rowan My name's Rowan. This is my friend, Martin.

Martin We're from Upper Lonsdale, sir.

Mack Upper Lonsdale? You've come some distance, then?

Rowan We were taken by the Guardians yesterday.

There is general surprise among the Outlaws

Mack You were taken by the Guardians, you say? What are you doing here if you were taken by the Guardians?

Rowan We escaped. We were taken to the Castle but we got away in the dark.

Martin That's right, sir. That's why we're here. There's nowhere else for us to go.

Mack If you escaped you're the first ever to do so. No-one who's been taken to the Castle has ever got out again.

Rowan But you've got to believe us! We were there! We saw the Eye! You've got to believe us!

Mack The Eye? You saw the Eye of Gondôr?

Martin It was awful, sir. It glows and throbs and makes a noise. And it makes you ill, sir.

Rowan And there's Brasov—he's a nasty piece of work. Then there's Kafka. He's out now, looking for the Stranger. And there's—

Mack What did you say? The Stranger?

Rowan That's right. The Stranger who came to Upper Lonsdale last week. He's got the Guardians worried, he has. Kafka's out looking for him now.

Mack I've heard about this Stranger. He was in Little Brumley when the Guardians came for the harvest. They couldn't have known he was there if they're still looking for him.

2nd Outlaw Take cover, everyone. Someone else is coming!

Everyone takes cover

Will and Stout, with the Stranger, enter

Mack Will! Stout! What are you doing here? Who's this you've brought with you?

Will Dad, this Stranger came to the Village looking for somewhere to stay.

Stout He was there when the Guardians came.

Mack Well, Stranger. We've been hearing about you. You seem to have brought some excitement to our Valley. My name's Mack. Welcome to our camp. It's not very comfortable, I'm afraid. But it's safe.

Stranger Thank you. I'm beginning to feel a little tired after all my travelling. Somewhere safe for the night will do very nicely.

Mack Sit down. (*To the Outlaws*) Come on, everybody. Back to work. (*To Jonah and Scamp*) You two—get on with those potatoes. We want to eat tonight. Will, go and get some wine for our guest. (*To the Stranger*) Now, Stranger. Tell us something about yourself. Who are you? How did you get into the Valley without being caught by the Guardians? What are you doing here?

Stranger Hold on! Hold on! That's enough to keep me going all night. (*He pauses*) I come from the north and I've been travelling for half a year now. As for getting into the Valley I just walked in. I'm interested to hear, though, about these Guardians of yours. Something to do with the Eye of Gondôr?

Mack That's right, Stranger. The Eye of Gondôr. And its Castle stands on the other side of the forest. The Eye has had power over this Valley since the Ancient Times, and the Guardians are its servants.

Stranger Why do you wear an Eye on your clothing?

Mack We always have, Stranger. Nobody asks why. We just do. It's the custom in the Valley. After all, it is the Eye that governs us.

Stranger Has anyone seen this Eye?

Big Harry Seen it! Seen it? No-one's ever seen it, Stranger. It's in the Castle. No-one's gone in there and come out alive, until today, that is.

Stranger Until today?

Rowan We've seen it, Stranger. It exists all right.

Stranger Who are you?

Rowan I'm Rowan. I come from Upper Lonsdale. You were there last week. Remember?

Stranger Oh yes. It was the first village.

Rowan And thanks to you the Guardians came. They took six of us but Martin and I managed to get away. If it hadn't been for you we'd have been at home now.

Martin Don't blame him, Rowan. If the Stranger hadn't been there the Guardians would have come for another reason. You know that. They never leave us alone for long.

Stranger What about the rest of you? Why are you outlawed? What have you done?

Big Harry Done? Done? We done nothing, that's what we done!

Mack Some of us are here because we couldn't pay our taxes, and some of us are here because we tried to save our folk from being taken by the Guardians.

Stranger And if you went back to your villages?

Mack Then the Guardians would take us.

Stranger To the Castle?

Mack To the Castle. (*Briskly*) Anyway . . . that's enough for now. (*To Jonah and Scamp*) You two scallywags! Is supper ready yet?

Jonah Won't be long, Mack.

Jonah and Scamp clear away the potatoes

Mack Come on, Stranger. And Rowan and Martin. You're our guests. It's time to eat.

There is general activity as the outlaws seat themselves for supper. Using their hands they eat bread, meat, fruit, etc

Come on, Stranger. Some wine! (*He pours some wine into a goblet*)

Stranger Your health!

Mack And yours. Now! Tell us what's going on outside the Valley. News is hard to come by. Come on! What's been happening?

Plenty of conversation goes on. There are occasional guffaws as jokes are told. There is backslapping and much merriment

Kafka enters stealthily and watches as the Outlaws eat

Big Harry (*standing*) Now listen everybody! Listen!

The noise dies down

I've been doing some thinking.

1st Outlaw That must have taken some doing!

There are guffaws from the Outlaws

Big Harry Very funny, very funny. Now just you listen. This is serious. It's about the Guardians.

Kafka draws closer, remaining hidden

They've stolen all the harvest.

2nd Outlaw We know that, Big Harry.

Big Harry Just sit and listen, will yer? Just sit and listen. (*He waits for silence*) We gotta do something about it, not just sit around all the time. We gotta do something.

2nd Outlaw And what do you suggest, Big Harry? Get it back?

There is general laughter

Big Harry (*becoming angry*) Shut up, will yer! Shut up! (*He waits for silence*) Why don't we *try* to get it back, eh? Why don't we try?

Mack That's a tall order, Big Harry. You're talking about the Guardians, you know. No-one can beat the Guardians, you know.

Rowan We did, Mack. We got away—remember?

Mack They've got the power of the Eye as well ...

Big Harry I know all about that, but as I see it, our families are going to starve without grain this winter. They're going to starve. And as young Rowan says, there might be a chance ...

Mack What are you suggesting, Big Harry?

Big Harry Well, firstly, as I see it, we're gonna die one way or the other.

Mack It may not come to that.

Big Harry What else will it come to? Where else are we gonna get food from? We can't get it from outside the Valley, so it has to come from inside. What happens when our stocks are used up?

1st Outlaw He's got a point there, Mack. There's not enough grain in the Village to feed everybody through the winter.

2nd Outlaw And if stocks are used up for eating, there's nothing left for sowing in the spring. That means no harvest next year either.

Big Harry As I see it, we gotta do something about getting our grain back, Guardians or no Guardians.

Mack You know what that means, don't you? (*He pauses*) It means an attack on the Castle.

Big Harry Well, we gotta try. We gotta try! (*He sits down*)

Mack (*standing*) Well, you've heard what Big Harry has said. He proposes an attack on the Castle of Gondôr—something no-one has ever done before, not since the Ancient Times. It's either that or, as Harry says, go hungry through the winter. It's up to you.

1st Outlaw Some of us have been outlaws for years. And what have we done? Nothing! We've relied on food from our families. Smuggling it to us has put them in danger. I'm for doing something for them.

2nd Outlaw Me too. We've got to try. We've got nothing to lose now.

Mack Is that how the rest of you feel?

Everyone murmurs general agreement

Anyone against?

There is silence

Kafka exits

Right. Get your weapons. We'll go tonight and hope that the Guardians
can't see too well in the dark.

The Outlaws disperse to collect weapons, clothing and so on

Will Dad. We're coming too.
Stout Yes, we're coming.
Mack No, lads. Someone's got to stay. If it goes wrong you've got to look
after your mother. There's no point in all of us getting caught. The
Guardians don't know you're involved. You get home.
Stranger And me?
Mack Look, Stranger. This is not your fight. I suggest you get out of this
Valley as soon as you can. Go back to where you came from (*Calling out*)
Right, men! We'll make for the Big Rocks first. Then we'll spy out the land.
(*To Will and Stout*) Right lads, back to the Village. And remember—you
know nothing of this. Not a word to anyone, not even your mother. Off
you go.

Will and Stout exit

Mack stands looking after them for a while, then turns to speak to the Stranger

Safe journey, Stranger. (*To the Outlaws*) Right, lads. Let's go.

The Outlaws and Mack exit

The Stranger stands staring after them

Stranger Safe journey to you, Mack, but I fear you'll be in the dungeons
before morning, and I can't do anything about it . . .

The Lights fade to a Black-out

SCENE 4

The Castle of Gondôr

*A table is set upon which are stacked old books. Some are open. Roth is reading
one of them*

Roth Written long ago . . . written long ago . . . he said it was written long
ago! I can't see anything in the old writings that can explain this Stranger.
There's nothing here! (*He slams the book shut in disgust*) Well, my dear
Eye? What do you make of it? Who is this Stranger? How can he just
appear and disappear at will? (*To himself*) For years I have ruled this
Valley. The secret of the Eye has been passed to me . . . to me! I rule! I have
the power! And my power is the power of fear: the Guardians fear me and
obey. The people fear them and obey! That's the way it's always been. And
now decay is setting in: there's rebellion in the air, and there's a Stranger in
the Valley who has no fear—and it is I who am beginning to fear him!

Brasov enters

Brasov My Lord.

Roth Well, what is it?

Brasov I've ... er ... interviewed the other prisoners we brought in and none of them knows anything about this Stranger.

Roth None of them?

Brasov None, my Lord.

Roth You stay here while I see if there are any more books in the vaults.

Roth exits

Brasov looks at the books and leafs through some of them

Kafka enters

Kafka Is Roth here?

Brasov He's gone to the vaults to get some more books. All day he's been studying the ancient writings.

Kafka Has he got anywhere?

Brasov I don't think so the way he stormed off. He's scared.

Kafka Aren't you, Brasov?

Brasov Me? Scared? Don't ask me if I'm scared, Kafka! Would you like to taste some of my "hospitality" downstairs?

Kafka Don't threaten me, Brasov! There's enough trouble in the Valley without you creating more! If you exercise just a little more patience you'll be able to extend your "hospitality" to quite a few more guests before the night's out.

Brasov What do you mean?

Roth enters with some more books

Roth Yes, Kafka. What do you mean?

Kafka My Lord Roth. I mean that the Outlaws are planning a raid on the Castle tonight.

Roth A raid on the Castle? Really? Our little plan to lure the Outlaws into the open seems to have worked. And the Stranger?

Kafka He's with them, but I don't think he'll come on the raid. He knows more than he lets on, that one. There's something very unusual about him. I can't make it out.

Roth And those prisoners we allowed to escape?

Kafka They made their way to the Outlaws' camp just as we thought and now they're on their way back again.

Roth Well, then, we should keep their cell warm for them, shouldn't we? Shall we prepare a welcome for our guests?

Brasov But, my Lord. What about the Stranger?

Roth What about him?

Brasov Well, my Lord. He's still free.

Roth One thing at a time, my dear Brasov. Let's deal with our little raiding party shall we? And I have some more reading to do!

Roth, Brasov and Kafka exit

The Lights fade to a Black-out

SCENE 5

Outside the Castle walls. That evening

The stage is bare. Nothing can be heard but the occasional owl hoot

The Outlaws enter stealthily

Mack (*quietly*) Well, we're here.
Big Harry It's all very quiet.
Mack Rowan—how do we get in?
Rowan There's a gate somewhere but that's guarded. There's a small door in the wall, though, but I don't know which way it is.
Mack Jonah! Scamp! Come here!

Jonah and Scamp appear

Jonah, you go that way (*pointing off left*) and see if you can find a door. Scamp, you go that way (*pointing off right*). We'll wait until you get back.

Jonah and Scamp exit

Big Harry It's creepy, Mack. It's creepy.
Mack There's no going back now, Harry. I reckon they must know we're here.
Rowan If they do they must be waiting, just to see what we do.
Martin Maybe they'll wait until we get inside?
Mack We just have to hope, that's all. What else have we got—only hope and a trusty sword arm.

There is a throbbing sound, menacing and oppressive. The Outlaws are startled and frightened. The Lights begin to throb with the sounds

Guardians appear out of the shadows

The action becomes slow motion as the Guardians raise their arms and point towards the Outlaws. Slowly the Outlaws clap their hands over their ears and in great pain begin to collapse. The Guardians stand perfectly still

Roth appears UC *with arms upraised*

Roth looks down on the Outlaws and speaks in a low, menacing voice whilst the throbbing continues

Roth So! You dare to approach the Castle of Gondôr? I am Roth, the Master of the Eye.
Mack (*in great pain*) You stole our harvest! Our people will starve without food!
Roth The people serve the Guardians! That is their function! That is your function!
Mack We are free men!
Roth No—you are not! You are servants of the Guardians. (*He sees Rowan and Martin*) Ah! Our young friends from Upper Lonsdale! How nice of you to return so soon! We've been expecting you. Drop your weapons!

The Outlaws, as if in a trance, leave their weapons on the ground and straighten up again, all in slow motion. The Guardians pick the weapons up

Now, tell me. Where is the Stranger?

No-one speaks

Don't be shy. You will tell me sooner or later. Where is the Stranger?

Again, no-one speaks. Suddenly the throbbing grows louder. The Outlaws experience a sharp pain. They slowly collapse with choking cries

Now, my friends. Who will tell me—where is the Stranger?

Mack We ... left ... him ... in the ... forest! In ... the ... forest!

The noise subsides. So does the pain

Roth Thank you. Now, my friends ... you wanted to enter the Castle. Be our guests! Don't be afraid. Come!

Still in a trance, and in slow motion, the Outlaws exit with the Guardians

The Light fades on Roth

Roth leaves the Stage

Jonah and Scamp enter nervously from opposite sides of the stage

Jonah Did ... you ... see ... what I saw?
Scamp What ... did ... you ... see?
Jonah The Guardians ...
Scamp ... and they've ... taken ... everybody ... prisoner ...
Jonah Let's get away from here!
Scamp All right! I'm coming!

CURTAIN

ACT II

The Market Square of Little Brumley. The following morning

The Storyteller is sweeping the ground. He notices the Audience, stops sweeping and comes DC *to lean on his broom*

Storyteller Hello, again. Today's the day of the big dance. At least, it's supposed to be, but now the Guardians have taken our harvest I don't know what we'll do. We'll get by, though. We can dance even if we've got no food, can't we? By the way, you went off to see the Outlaws, didn't you? How did you get on? They're a fine bunch of lads. Of course, they're not what *we* would call Outlaws. I mean they haven't done anything wrong. It's just that the Guardians took a disliking to them. Now that they're Outlaws means that we're not allowed any contact, you see, but between you and me, the villagers supply them with all their food, otherwise they'd starve—you know what I mean? You can't grow anything in the forest, after all's said and done. Some of them have been there for years. I don't know how they stand it, really I don't. Still, the trees keep the Guardians out. That's a bonus, I suppose. (*He listens*) Hey! The Village is waking up. I'd better get on and sweep the square.

Villagers enter, some carrying brooms, some buckets and rags, some mops

They start to clean up the square; some hang up bunting for the dance

Will (*wearily*) Somehow my heart just isn't in it.
Stout I feel like that too.
Will How can we have a harvest dance when we've got no harvest?
Stout (*confidentially*) I wonder how Dad and the others got on at the Castle last night?
Will Yeah! Maybe we'll have a harvest after all!
Stout I wish I'd been there. Sock it to 'em, I would. A left and a right!
Will Watch out! Here comes the Mayor.

The Mayor enters and approaches Will and Stout

Mayor Good morning, Will. Good morning, Stout. You're cheerful today, I'm glad to see. Not like everybody else. Dear, dear me. Look at them! So sad! I mean, there's nothing to be gained in being miserable, is there? What's done is done. The Guardians have taken the harvest and that's that. We must carry on, keep our peckers up, eh?
Will Yes, Mr Mayor. If you say so.

Mayor I do say so, I do! Yes, we must try to be cheerful, to see the bright side of things. I expect the Guardians had a good reason for taking our harvest.

Will Mr Mayor! How on earth can you say a thing like that!

Mayor What, what? What do you mean, my boy?

Will How could the Guardians have a good reason for stealing our harvest? How could the Guardians have a good reason for stealing anything? I thought stealing was wrong—except when the Guardians do it, is that it? Anyway, our harvest belongs to us! If we don't get it back we'll starve!

Mayor Now, now, Will. Don't you trouble your young head about things like that. You leave that to us grown-ups. Yes, you leave things well alone.

Will But Mr Mayor—what are you going to do about it?

Stout Yes, Mr Mayor. What are you going to do? Are you going to ask for it back? Are you?

Mayor Well, young man. I don't know about that, oh no. You shouldn't ask such questions. They can get you into trouble, questions can. The Guardians rule this Valley. Don't you forget it. If we want to lead a quiet life we should do just as we're told and not interfere, that's what we should do.

Will But Mr Mayor—

Mayor No more buts, young man. I don't know what you're coming to, asking questions. No good ever came of asking questions. Just do as you're told, young man. Just do as you're told.

Stout But what are we gong to eat at the dance tonight, Mr Mayor?

Mayor I'm sure we'll think of something ... yes ... I'm sure we will.

Jonah and Scamp enter, very wearily

The Stranger enters but stands apart

A murmur goes up among the Villagers

Will (*alarmed*) What happened, Jonah? Scamp? Did you get the grain?

Stout How's Dad? Is he all right?

Jonah (*breathlessly*) Captured. They've all been captured.

Scamp The Guardians came and—it was awful!

Will (*shouting*) Tell us what happened! Is our dad all right?

Mayor Now, now, now! What's been going on, Jonah? Tell me ... what have you done?

Jonah Well, Mr Mayor, Mack and the others decided last night to go to the Castle and try and get your grain back.

Mayor Oh dear. A calamity! What have they done? What will the Guardians think? This is what comes of interfering. Oh dear!

Jonah Well, we had to do something, Mr Mayor. We couldn't just let you all starve this winter, could we?

Mayor Yes, my boy. It's very good of you to think of us, but we ought not to meddle, we ought not to meddle.

Stout Come on, Jonah. Tell us what happened!

All Come on! Tell us what happened! How's Mack? *etc*

Mayor Now calm down everybody. Everybody calm down. All right, boys. In your own words tell us exactly what happened.

The Villagers gather closer

Jonah Well, Big Harry said we ought to try and get our grain back from the Castle and everybody agreed. Rowan and Martin from Upper Lonsdale came with us. They'd been captured by the Guardians but had escaped, and they knew the way in.

There are murmurs of surprise from the crowd

1st Villager Escaped? From the Guardians? Never!
Jonah I tell you, they did.
Scamp That's right! We didn't believe it at first.
Jonah They knocked out a guard and escaped.
Scamp In the darkness.
Jonah And they made their way to the forest.
Scamp And met us at the camp.
1st Villager Well, who'd have believed it?
2nd Villager Maybe the Guardians aren't as invincible as we thought.
Mayor Now, now. No more of that. We don't want more trouble in Little Brumley. Go on, boys! Go on!
Jonah Well, when we all agreed, we set off for the Big Rocks.
Scamp Then we turned north towards the river and crossed at the ford.
Jonah We got to the Castle about midnight . . .
Scamp . . . and Mack sent Jonah and me to look for a door in the wall.
Jonah And while we were away the Guardians came. There was a horrible noise—it fair gave me a headache, it did.
Scamp When we got back everybody had been taken into the Castle!

The Stranger approaches

Stranger Good morning, everyone. I couldn't help hearing what you two said.
Mayor Oh, good morning. Well . . . I must confess . . . a lot does seem to have happened since you arrived.
Stranger Mr Mayor, would you mind if I asked the boys one or two questions?
Mayor I don't suppose that will do any harm but they do seem to have said everything.
Stranger Tell me, Jonah. When the Guardians appeared, what happened— exactly?
Jonah There was a noise, like we said.
Stranger What kind of noise?
Jonah A throbbing noise . . . a kind of booming noise. Heavy. It sort of gave you a headache.
Stranger Where do you think that noise came from?
Jonah I never really thought about that. It sort of came from all around you. It seemed to be in the air, really.
Stranger Then what?
Jonah Then the Guardians came and surrounded the men.
Stranger And then?

Jonah Then everybody sort of . . . collapsed.

Scamp That's right, they just fell down. That's when Roth appeared.

Stranger Roth? Tell me about Roth.

Scamp Well . . . he just appeared. On the wall of the Castle, he was. He said . . . what was it now? (*Searching for words*) He said "I am Roth . . . you dare to approach the Castle of Gondôr . . . I am Roth, the Master of the Eye" and then he went on to say that we were servants of the Guardians and he made everybody drop their weapons.

Stranger How did he do that?

Scamp Everybody seemed to be hypnotized. They just did it.

Jonah Very, very slowly. They all moved slowly.

Scamp Then he made everybody stand up and they walked into the Castle.

Stranger Where were you when all this was happening? I mean, how far away?

Scamp I was behind a tree.

Jonah I was behind a rock . . . ooh . . . about twenty yards away.

Stranger Thank you very much.

Mayor Well, Stranger, what does it mean? I'll tell you what it means—it means not to meddle, that's what it means!

Stranger (*addressing the crowd*) Does it not strike you as strange? First of all, there was no battle, no fighting; secondly, Mack and the others entered the Castle of their own free will; and thirdly the prisoners were taken alive. What does this suggest to you?

Mayor Suggest, sir. It suggests that we ought to keep out of it. It was folly even to think of attacking the Guardians. Why, it hasn't been done since the Ancient Times, not since the Ancient Times, it hasn't.

Stranger So it has been done, then?

Mayor Well, I suppose so, so the legends say.

Stranger You place much store in legends in this Valley, don't you?

Mayor (*proudly*) They're our history!

Stranger Precisely! Your history! But legends aren't your future. When are you people going to look forward instead of back? If you want to you can free yourselves of the Guardians. If you want to, you can free your menfolk captured last night!

Mayor It's all very well for you to speak like that, Stranger, but it's our Valley! We have to live in it. And we have to take the consequences if we disobey the Guardians.

Stranger And how many of you want to live here under the Guardians when you have the chance of throwing them off and being free?

The Villagers murmur among themselves

Will Stranger, exactly how can we rid ourselves of the Guardians?

Mayor Quiet! This is rebellion! I cannot have you talking like this! I am the Mayor and I forbid it!

1st Villager Come on, Mr Mayor. What choice have we got?

2nd Villager My family are going to starve this winter!

The Villagers' reactions grow louder and louder

Stranger How many of you are willing to come with me? How many of you are willing to rescue Mack and the others? How many of you are willing to fight for your freedom? How many?

There are cheers from the Villagers

Then listen to me.

The Villagers gather round

And I'll tell you what I'll do ...

The Lights fade to a Black-out

SCENE 2

The Castle of Gondôr

The Outlaws are in chains before the Eye

Martin Well, here we are again.

Rowan If we got out once we can get out again, Martin. Don't give up yet.

Martin Last time they weren't expecting anything; this time they'll be on their guard. There's no chance of escape now.

Rowan Don't give up hope! Look on the bright side—gruel three times a day, exciting company, a roof over your head.

Martin It's not funny, Rowan.

Rowan It's not hopeless, Martin! I have one thought, Martin. And that's to get out of here or die in the trying. Keep your eyes and ears open and the chance will come.

Martin But the guards—

Rowan The guards? Look, Martin. The initiative is with us. They don't know if we're going to make a move and they don't know when, so they have to watch us all the·time. The advantage is with us because they know we *can* get out of this wretched Castle, and they know they *can* be beaten.

Mack He's right, you know. You got out once—that must really hurt their pride. They're watching us keenly, but they can't keep it up indefinitely. They've got to sleep and they've got to change the guards sometime. Our chance will come.

1st Outlaw I wonder what's happening back in Little Brumley?

2nd Outlaw Preparing for the dance tonight, I shouldn't wonder.

1st Outlaw Without any harvest?

2nd Outlaw That won't stop them. You know Will is sweet on Mistress Marion, don't you?

1st Outlaw Aye, I heard about that. It's true—you don't need a harvest to go courtin'.

2nd Outlaw It's months since I went to a dance. Midsummer's Day, in fact. I slipped down to Little Brumley after sunset so that the Guardians wouldn't know I'd left the forest. It was great. I wonder what Mistress Elizabeth is doing now?

Big Harry Helping my wife, I hope.

Mack Why's that, Harry?

Big Harry She always does, that's why. She always does when it comes to a dance or suchlike. She's very good, is Mistress Elizabeth. Always lends a helping hand.

Mack That's the nice thing about Little Brumley.

Big Harry What's that, then, Mack?

Mack Lending a helping hand.

Martin Folk do that in Upper Lonsdale too. Real friendly they are.

Rowan And it's the Guardians who cast the shadow—let's not forget that. That's why we're here, isn't it—because of their shadow.

Big Harry But the Guardians have always been around, Rowan. It's the way things are.

Rowan It's the way things are! It's the way things are because you've always let things stay the way they are. It's been the tradition since the Ancient Times but does it always have to be so? You know, I used to tend my Dad's sheep up on the high pasture above our Village, and when I was walking I'd feel the wind on my face and I'd see the birds flying free in the sky. They didn't fear the Guardians. I used to wonder about that. Why didn't the birds fear the Eye? Why didn't the sheep? Why is it that only people fear this thing?

Big Harry But we tried, didn't we? And look where we are—imprisoned in the Castle. I mean, we did try.

Mack And we'll try again, Harry, don't you worry. Rowan's right. We've let things drift on and never asked ourselves the important questions.

Martin You're forgetting one thing.

Mack What's that, Martin?

Martin When the Guardians caught us, that noise. We couldn't beat it. We gave in without a fight. The Eye does have power.

Mack I've been thinking about that but I can't make it out. What made us freeze like that?

Big Harry I couldn't move a muscle.

Mack Neither could I, and it wasn't for the want of trying. And neither could you, Rowan, for all your hatred of the Guardians. We all came here determined to fight and they beat us hands down.

Big Harry It's the Eye where the power comes from, that's where it comes.

Roth, Brasov and Kafka enter

Roth You're right, my friend. It's the great Eye of Gondôr that has power, and here you all are, you who dared to challenge the authority of the Guardians of the Eye!

Mack And we're still a challenge, aren't we? What are you going to do to us?

Roth At the moment? Precisely nothing. No, we're interested in a far greater prize. We're interested in the Stranger. Soon, he will be here with you. When we have him there will be no challenge whatsoever.

Mack Why is he so important to you? He's just a traveller.

Roth He's no traveller, my friend. He's a threat. He didn't come into this

Valley by chance, oh no. He's here for a purpose, and I am most interested in finding out precisely what that purpose is.

Rowan So go and get him, Roth!

Roth Lord Roth!! You will address me as Lord Roth or it will be the worse for you! Brasov, teach our young friend some respect.

Kafka grabs Rowan from behind, pinioning his arms. Brasov hits Rowan who collapses to the ground

There will be respect in this Valley! There will be obedience in this Valley! Brasov!

Brasov hits one of the Outlaws who collapses in pain, then he hits another

There is a spirit of rebellion in this Valley. It will be crushed. Our young friend here (*pointing to Rowan*) speaks of hope—there is no hope! You entertain hopes of escape—there will be no escape. His escape yesterday was no accident, my friends; it was no credit to him. It was my way of luring you out of the forest. And here you all are! I am the Master! I will not be challenged and I will not be threatened! Don't place any hope in the Stranger. He is one man, one man against the might and power of the Eye of Gondôr. There will be no change in this Valley. I have spoken! Kafka!

Kafka My Lord?

Roth The Stranger is in Little Brumley. Disguise yourself as a villager, go there and find out what his plans are. And find out who else is involved. Take care that your disguise is . . . perfect!

Kafka Yes, my Lord. With pleasure.

Kafka exits

Roth Come, Brasov. We'll leave our friends here to nurse their bruises, and their broken spirits!

Roth and Brasov exit

Rowan I—will—beat—him. I promise. I will beat him! My spirit isn't broken, I don't care what he says!

Mack But he has the upper hand now, Rowan. There's not much we can do while he's got us in chains.

Martin There's not a lot we could do even if we weren't in chains. There's still the Eye.

Mack And there are a lot of people in the Valley who are content with the way it's always been. Not everyone will want to fight the Guardians. It's hard to make people change . . .

Rowan Even if they're starving?

Mack Even if they're starving. They're good people, don't get me wrong, but some will want to get by as best they can. They just want to lead a quiet life. Rebels are always in the minority, Rowan. Fighters are few and far between.

Rowan Maybe it only takes a few, eh? Maybe it will only take us?

Mack Maybe so, but just at the moment there's little we can do. Let's hope that if the Stranger has come to this Valley with a purpose he achieves it, whatever it might be. Somehow I have a feeling our hopes lie with him . . .

The Lights fade to a Black-out

SCENE 3

The Market Square of Little Brumley

The action is continuous from the end of Act II, Scene 2 but the Villagers are "frozen" while the Storyteller speaks

Storyteller This is a fine how-do-you-do! The Stranger has put the cat among the pigeons now! Who'd have thought it? Only yesterday we were preparing for our harvest dance, as normal as you please, and today we're threatened with starvation, the Outlaws are in the Castle dungeons and the Stranger is calling for an uprising! (*He pauses*) Exciting, isn't it?

Everyone comes to life again

Will Stranger, I don't quite understand you. Exactly how can we rid ourselves of the Guàrdians?

Stranger The first thing to do is to find the source of their power.

Mayor But we know that! It's the Eye.

Stranger That's what you've always believed, but that's where you're wrong.

Mayor Wrong? Wrong? Oh dear me, how can that be wrong?

Stranger Mr Mayor, it's not the Eye that's the source of their power—it's you!

Mayor Me? Me? I'm the source of their power? How dare you—

Stranger No, Mr Mayor. Don't misunderstand me. It's not you personally. It's everyone.

Will I still don't understand you, Stranger.

Stranger Now, think! You all believe in the power of the Eye. When the Guardians say they have power over you you all believe them. For generations you have taught your children to fear the Guardians and for generations you *have* feared the Guardians. And all the time you believe it the Guardians are safe.

Kafka, disguised as a Villager, enters and stands nearby

Stout Do you mean to say that we're being hoodwinked? That we've been hoodwinked all these years?

Stranger That's exactly what I mean. You are the slaves of your own fear, no more and no less.

Mayor Why, this is preposterous! Nonsense! I've never heard anything so ridiculous in all my life!

Stranger Mr Mayor. What could be more ridiculous than believing in an Eye that none of you has ever seen in a Castle that none of you has ever entered?

Mayor But the Guardians! What about them? We've seen them all right.

Stranger The strength of their power is in the strength of your fear.

Stout My Dad didn't fear them and look what happened to him!

Stranger No, he didn't fear them when he was safe in the forest, but when he came face to face with them then his fear got the better of him! But there is a way of defeating them!
Will How's that, then Stranger?
All Yes, how? Tell us! *etc, etc*
Stranger Listen! Listen! All of you! (*He pauses for silence*) The first battle you have to win is the battle with yourselves. You must take off your Eye badges.

There is consternation and cries of What? Never! etc

If you are resolved not to fear the Eye and not to fear the Guardians then why wear their badge? It's a badge of fear. Tear it off. (*To Will*) How about it, Will? Will you be the first? Tear it off!

Will looks at his badge and he looks at the Stranger. He brings his hands up. His actions reflect his inner struggle

Will I can't! I can't! I've always worn this badge, ever since I was a child. It's part of me! I just can't do it!
Stranger Yes you can, Will. Your fear of the Eye is a fear of your own making. You chose to fear—now choose not to. If you win this battle you'll win all battles! Go on! Tear it off! Go on!

Will finally tears off his badge. The Villagers gasp, some with shock, some with surprise

Now how about you, Stout? Take off your badge. You don't belong to the Guardians any more!

Stout goes through a similar process before pulling off his badge. Will cheers him and together they throw their badges on the ground. Then the Stranger, Will and Stout go through the crowd encouraging the others to do the same. They all do so, except the Mayor

Stranger Now, Mr Mayor. It's your turn. Will you tear off your badge?
Mayor Most certainly not. I've always worn my badge. It's the law. I can't give up my old ways just because a Stranger suddenly comes and tells us to.
Will But Mr Mayor! You're the only one wearing a badge now. You're the odd one out.
Stout Come on, Mr Mayor. What have you got to lose?
Mayor My freedom, that's what I've got to lose. My freedom. Just wait till the Guardians hear about this!
Stranger You're wrong, Mr Mayor. Your freedom is what you have to gain. At the moment you're the only slave in the Village. It's the Guardians' turn to fear now.

The Mayor looks round. As he does so the Villagers encourage him with shouts of: Come on, Mr Mayor! You can do it! etc, etc. After a long inner struggle his hands begin to move towards his badge. The struggle continues until he finally tears it free. The Villagers cheer

Kafka makes an inconspicuous exit

Stranger Now! Listen! (*He waits for the cheering to die down*) If we work together you can have your dance tonight, and your harvest, and your families.

The Villagers all cheer

The first thing you need is weapons—anything you can lay your hands on—pitchforks, knives, hoes, brooms. Anything. Off you go! We meet back here in half an hour!

With much excitement the Villagers exit, except the Storyteller

Storyteller Exciting, isn't it? Now, what shall I take? I could use this broom, I suppose. What do you think? I can't wait to get started. There's something new happening in this Valley; there's a smell of change in the air. Still, I can't help wondering what the Guardians are going to make of all this . . .

The Storyteller exits

The Lights fade to a Black-out

SCENE 4

Another part of the Castle

Roth and Kafka are talking

Roth Ah, Kafka. What's the news?
Kafka It's bad, my Lord.
Roth Well, tell me!
Kafka The Stranger has all the Villagers on his side. They're marching to the Castle.
Roth We've met that little problem before. We'll prepare our usual warm welcome!
Kafka That may not be so easy this time, my Lord. The people have removed their badges.
Roth What?!
Kafka The Stranger is very clever. He knows our weakness.
Roth He is clever indeed. So the people think they have lost their fear, do they? Wait until they approach the Castle—we'll see if we can't remind them what real fear is. Come, Kafka! I have a little plan!

Roth and Kafka exit

The Lights fade to a Black-out

SCENE 5

Near the Castle

The Villagers, all carrying weapons of some sorts, enter, led by the Stranger

Stranger Keep together. Don't straggle.
Mayor How much further? My old legs won't carry me.
Will Don't worry, Mr Mayor. Just you wait until we meet the Guardians.
  You'll be all right then.
Mayor Meeting the Guardians is just what I'm worrying about.

*There is a clap of thunder and a burst of lightning. It continues. Action goes to
slow motion to emphasize the length of the journey*

Stranger Don't be afraid. Stay together.

*The journey to the Castle takes the form of a slow motion circle on the stage.
The thunder fades to be replaced by sundry eerie noises: maniacal laughter, a
whistling wind, animal's roar, etc*

  (*Standing erect and waving the Villagers on*) Don't listen! They're only
  tricks to frighten you!
Stout They're succeeding! Ohhh!

Eventually all the noises fade to silence

  Roth and Kafka appear at the edge of the stage, unseen by the Villagers

Roth It's not working! They should be terrified by now!
Kafka I told you the Stranger was clever.
Roth I'll show him who's clever!

  Roth and Kafka exit

The journey continues

Stranger Not far to go now. We're almost there!

Further eerie sounds are heard

  Monsters and Spirits enter to haunt the Villagers

Stranger Don't look at them! They don't exist! They are only figments of
  your imaginations! Keep your heads down. Don't look at them! (*He
  repeats himself as long as is necessary to calm the Villagers*)

  The Monsters and Spirits exit and the sounds die away

  Roth and Kafka appear as before

Roth And still they come!
Kafka What next, my Lord?
Roth We wait—until they reach the Castle. We'll see how brave they are
  when they meet—the Guardians!

  Roth and Kafka exit

The journey continues

Jonah This is it! This is where Mack and the others were captured.
Scamp I'm scared.

The Villagers look round. They are scared too

Stranger Now listen everybody. Whatever happens, do exactly as I say. Don't go off by yourself—stay close. And whatever you see, remember—they're counting on your fear to win the battle.

As before there is a throbbing sound, menacing and oppressive. The Villagers are startled. The Lights begin to throb with the sound

The Guardians appear out of the shadows

The Guardians raise their arms and point to the Villagers who clap their hands over their ears and slowly begin to collapse in great pain

Roth appears

Roth I am Roth! Who dares approach the Castle of Gondôr?
Stranger Don't look at the Guardians! Don't listen!

The Stranger rushes round the company, encouraging them when they falter. Some look at the ground, some are tempted to look at the Guardians

Guardians (*chanting*) Look at us! Look at us! Look at us! Gondôr! Gondôr! Gondôr! (*and so on*)
Stranger Don't look! Don't look! Look at the ground!

The battle goes on, and as the struggle for the Villagers continues, more and more people look at the ground and become perfectly still

As this happens the Guardians slowly withdraw

The throbbing sound dies away until there is silence and stillness

Roth exits

Will We've won! We've won!

All the Villagers cheer and shout

Stranger Listen to me! (*He waits for quiet*) We haven't won yet. We are still outside the Castle. The Guardians are almost defeated, but they are not destroyed. We must find a way into the Castle.
Jonah If I remember rightly, the door is around that corner (*He points off*)
Stranger That's the way in then. Come on everyone!

Everyone exits

The Lights fade to Black-out

SCENE 6

The Castle of Gondôr

The Outlaws are chained as before

Roth, Brasov and Kafka enter

Roth (*to Kafka*) We are not finished yet! There is still the Eye!

Kafka But what good will that do? I'm the one who fears now!
Roth Fear? What does a Guardian know of fear? (*Pointing to the Outlaws*) It is they who must fear!
Rowan We don't fear you, Roth! You're finished! Why don't you give up now?

Brasov hits Rowan who collapses, dazed

Roth Stop snivelling, Kafka!
Kafka But the Stranger has entered the Castle! He'll be here any minute!
Roth Let him come. Let them all come! I don't care! The Eye will teach them!
Kafka But the Eye has no power, you know that! The Stranger is right—we rely on the people's own fear. We always have. And now they have no fear—but I do!

The Villagers enter, cheering, with some Guardians who are fighting a rearguard action

The Guardians are driven back and go to stand with Roth, Brasov and Kafka behind the Eye

Stranger Roth! The game is up! We demand your surrender!
Roth Surrender? Who are you to make demands, Stranger? It is I, Roth, who demands your surrender. People of the Valley—lay down your arms!

The people falter and look to the Stranger

Stranger They no longer fear you, Roth. You no longer have power over this Valley.
Roth No longer have power? People don't change, Stranger. They still fear, deep down inside—you can't change that. Watch!

Roth points to the Eye which begins to glow. The Guardians raise their arms and point to the Eye. As its light throbs so it is accompanied by dreadful sounds. It grows dark in the Castle, except for the light of the Eye. The Villagers react with horror

Stranger It's a trick! Look away! Look away!

The Stranger runs around making the Villagers look away from the Eye. They clap their hands over their ears and grit their teeth, feeling the pain but not giving in to it. The Stranger then forces his way among the Guardians until he finds a "cable" behind the Eye. He cuts it; there is a explosion, a flash and the Eye's light goes out. The noises fade. The Castle lights come up

All right, you can look now! See … it's a fake. That is your "Eye"!

The Guardians try to escape. They are caught. The Outlaws are freed from their chains and the Guardians chained in their place

Mack Well … it's all over, then?
Stranger All over. The Guardians only maintained their power because deep down inside you wanted them to. When you began to resist it was inevitable that their power should crumble away. Now that you know the truth about the so-called "Eye" you can be free from its influence.

Mack (*pointing to the Guardians*) What are we going to do about them?

Stranger That will be up to you. For now, I'd suggest you offer them the same hospitality they offered you. With them out of the way you can all go back to Little Brumley and enjoy that harvest dance, can't you?

Mayor That we can, Stranger. That we can!

Roth We nearly won, you know, Stranger.

Stranger Yes, Roth. You nearly did.

Roth Do you think the people have lost their fear? When it came to the crunch they needed you, didn't they?

Stranger But they won, Roth. In the end they won. You can never take that away.

Roth And if a new fear replaces the old?

Stranger Then they'll know what to do, won't they? (*To the Villagers*) Tomorrow you've got decisions to make, but today? Today is harvest! Today we dance!

The Villagers cheer then the action is frozen as the Storyteller slowly makes his way through the tableau

Storyteller So there we are: the end of the story. Tonight we dance after all. Young Will will be chasing Mistress Marion; Stout will have eyes on Mistress Lucy. Tomorrow Rowan and Martin will go back to Upper Lonsdale and watch the sheep on the high pasture. The Outlaws can go home again and sit by their firesides. And me? Well, as I told you, I rather fancy Mistress Rachel . . . aaah! A lot has happened when you think of it, ever since the Stranger arrived. We never did find out who he really was, at least not until a long while after . . . when we read it in the Ancient Writings. But this is where our story ends. Goodnight!

CURTAIN

PRODUCTION NOTES

The Set
The Evil Eye of Gondôr was originally written for performance in a school hall with audience on three sides. It could as easily be performed on a conventional stage, but a simple set with the scenes suggested just by the props works well.

For example, in the original production we had a black set with two long strips of yellow material no more than half a metre wide hanging down against a black back wall, and on to that set we brought a red table for Roth (Act I, Scene 4) and a yellow table and benches for the forest scene (Act I, Scene 3). Books, food, wine and other small props were brought on by the cast.

The Eye
Above the stage hung the **Eye**. It was there all the time, all-seeing, all-knowing, malevolently watching. Actually, it was a concave metal dish about a metre across, covered in foil on which two spotlights shone during the throbbing eye scenes. The eye motif was also painted onto the back wall. Producers will find other ways of creating the eye, but the point is that the forces of oppression which it represents are always on the watch, no matter who or what they are.

It's important, therefore, that the **Eye Badges** the people wear are uniform; they are badges imposed by the oppressors, symbols of the people's subservience and fear. They should be quite large and might look something like the illustration. They can be made out of two colours of felt (we used red and black), and attached to the **Villagers'** and **Outlaws'** costumes by velcro-strip which is easily torn off and easily put back again for the next performance.

The **Guardians** should also wear eye badges, but Roth's might have some variation of size and shape. The motif might also be useful for tickets and programmes, or for hanging around the auditorium.

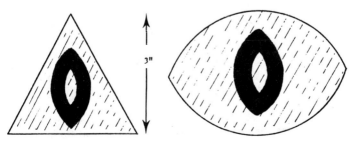

Effects

The Sound Recordist can have a lot of fun inventing the throbbing noise of the Evil Eye. It needs to be built up over a layer of regular throbs or beats with at least one layer of high-pitched sound. Other effects are much more straightforward. Some of them could be played live if you have instrumentalists available.

The Lighting Team will need to practise the lighting that goes with the sounds so that it is synchronized as much as possible. If the Evil Eye hangs over the stage they should try to get some reflection into the audience.

When the Stranger destroys the power of the Evil Eye there needs to be quite an explosion. After all, he is destroying the means by which dictators all over the world impose their will. It's a momentous occasion, one that should stand in the memory.

FURNITURE AND PROPERTY LIST

See also Production Notes

Essential properties only are listed here. Further items can be added at the Producer's discretion

ACT I
SCENE 1

On stage: Sacks
Farm implements

Off stage: Tools **(Will)**
Sack **(Stout)**

SCENE 2

Set: Eye of Gondôr
Personal: **Guard:** sword, cloak

SCENE 3

Set: Outlaws' camp—clothes, weapons, potatoes, pot, knives, table set with bread, meat, fruit, goblets, wine, etc.

SCENE 4

Strike: Camp

Set: Table. *On it:* books
Off stage: Books **(Roth)**

SCENE 5

Strike: Table
Personal: **Outlaws:** weapons

ACT II
SCENE 1

Off stage: Brooms, buckets, rags, mops, bunting, etc. **(Villagers)**
Personal: **Storyteller:** broom

SCENE 2

No properties required

SCENE 3

Personal: **Storyteller:** broom

SCENE 4

No properties required

SCENE 5

Personal: **Villagers:** weapons

SCENE 6

No properties required

LIGHTING PLOT

Various interior and exterior settings. No practical fittings required

ACT I, SCENE 1
To open: Outdoor lighting, early evening

Cue 1   **2nd Villager:** "And don't . . . come . . . back."   (Page 4)
              Lights fade

Cue 2   As **Guardians** enter   (Page 4)
              Dull, mysterious lighting

Cue 3   **Guardians** exit   (Page 4)
              Revert to previous lighting

Cue 4   As Bell tolls   (Page 5)
              Twilight effect

Cue 5   **Will**, **Stout** and **Stranger** tiptoe off   (Page 6)
              Fade to Black-out

ACT I, SCENE 2
To open: Sinister, interior lighting. Eye glows

Cue 6   **Roth** moves behind Eye   (Page 9)
              Eye fades and glows as general lighting fades

Cue 7   When ready   (Page 9)
              Lights revert to previous level

Cue 8   **Roth** and **Brasov** exit at end of scene   (Page 11)
              Fade to Black-out

ACT I, SCENE 3
To open: Exterior lighting. Evening

Cue 9   **Stranger:** ". . . do anything about it."   (Page 17)
              Lights fade to Black-out

ACT I, SCENE 4
To open: Interior lighting

Cue 10   **Roth**, **Brasov** and **Kafka** exit   (Page 18)
              Fade to Black-out

ACT I, SCENE 5
To open: Exterior lighting. Night

Cue 11   **Mack:** ". . . trusty sword arm."   (Page 19)
              Light throbs with sound

Cue 12   **Outlaws** exit with **Guardians**   (Page 20)
            Throbbing light fades, leaving dull lighting

ACT II, SCENE 1
To open: Morning light

Cue 13   **Stranger:** "... what I'll do."   (Page 25)
            Fade to Black-out

ACT II, SCENE 2
To open: Interior lighting

Cue 14   **Mack:** "... hopes lie with him ..."   (Page 28)
            Fade to Black-out

ACT II, SCENE 3
To open: Exterior lighting

Cue 15   **Storyteller** exits   (Page 30)
            Fade to Black-out

ACT II, SCENE 4
To open: Interior lighting

Cue 16   **Roth:** "I have a little plan!"   (Page 30)
            Fade to Black-out

ACT II, SCENE 5
To open: Exterior lighting

Cue 17   **Mayor:** "... just what I'm worrying about."   (Page 31)
            Lighning

Cue 18   As throbbing begins   (Page 32)
            Lights throb with sound. Continue until ready to cease

Cue 19   As **Villagers** and **Stranger** exit   (Page 32)
            Fade to Black-out

ACT II, SCENE 6
To open: Exterior lighting

Cue 20   **Roth:** "... you can't change that. Watch!"   (Page 33)
            Eye glows. Decrease general lighting

Cue 21   As "cable" breaks   (Page 33)
            Eye light snaps off. General lighting reverts to previous level

EFFECTS PLOT

ACT I

MADE AND PRINTED IN GREAT BRITAIN BY
LATIMER TREND & COMPANY LTD PLYMOUTH
MADE IN ENGLAND